Original title:
The Point of Life (It's Somewhere Around Here)

Copyright © 2025 Creative Arts Management OÜ
All rights reserved.

Author: Colin Harrington
ISBN HARDBACK: 978-1-80566-218-1
ISBN PAPERBACK: 978-1-80566-513-7

Twilight Moments

In twilight hues, the world can dance,
With quirky clouds that prance and prance.
A cat in shades, with a sunhat on,
Sips lemonade while the night goes on.

A bug on a log, with a fiddler's bow,
Plays a tune to make the flowers grow.
The fireflies join in a light ballet,
Creating magic as night turns to day.

The Road of Resilience

A rubber chicken leads the way,
Mocking struggles that hold at bay.
With goofy grins, we wade through muck,
In puddles deep, we find our luck.

Each bump ahead, we choose to ride,
In silly hats, we won't subside.
The road will twist, but we'll stay bold,
With laughter's weight, we'll break the mold.

Seeds of Inspiration

A squirrel with dreams of gourmet cheese,
Digs up hope with utmost ease.
In every nut, a future bright,
Sprouted silliness takes flight.

With each forgetful gardener's frown,
We've grown a crop of giggles brown.
In the dirt and mess, we plant some cheer,
And make confetti from doubt and fear.

Embracing the Moment

A sock that's lost, now on a spree,
Chased by dust bunnies, wild and free.
Each giggle shared is a silly gift,
As we embrace life's little rift.

With friendly waves from a broomstick knight,
We hop along, in pure delight.
Life's a chuckle, a wink, a jest,
In goofy mischief, we are the best.

Between Dreams and Reality

In slippers made of marshmallow,
I wander where the wild things trot,
Chasing shadows of a sparrow,
But slipping on the thoughts I forgot.

The cat is plotting world domination,
With lasers in its playful gaze,
While I search for a grand revelation,
Hidden in yesterday's maze.

Balancing on toes made of fluff,
I dance with clouds in a dizzy spin,
Trying to find the right kind of stuff,
To make sense of where I begin.

In a cereal box, I find my muse,
With spoons to sprinkle stars on toast,
Life's quirks are the best kind of blues,
That keep me laughing, more or less.

Flickering Insights

I once thought wisdom wore glasses,
Instead, it's wearing polka dots,
It trips on truths and slightly crashes,
The punchline's always what it's got.

In coffee stains I seek my answers,
Dancing across my morning brew,
The spoon dives in like wild prancers,
And serves me revelations askew.

A lightbulb flickers in my mind,
But flickers sometimes lose their spark,
Yet in the chaos, I'm inclined,
To laugh at all the wild remarks.

My dreams are noodles, long and sleek,
Twisted in the broth of the day,
With every sip, I lose my streak,
But find a joke that's here to stay.

Roots Beneath the Surface

The trees gossip about my shoes,
Trading whispers with the breeze,
They think my socks are old news,
Yet, beneath they share their keys.

Worms conduct underground affairs,
Debating fruits and veggies too,
While I sit up here in my cares,
Wondering just what I should do.

Digging deeper in the soil,
Found a sock from two years past,
It's quite the treasure, full of oil,
Turns out life's a quirky cast.

Rabbits with their secret maps,
Show shortcuts through the garden maze,
A life without the known mishaps,
Is just a purple haze of days.

The Language of Moments

Lost in a moment, I find a word,
Dancing like a chicken on parade,
It chirps and twirls, quite absurd,
And I giggle at the jumbled charade.

Time tickles clocks with its funny hands,
While I scribble thoughts on napkins set,
It's a language only laughter understands,
Making sense in a jolly duet.

The cat interrupts, strikes a pose,
Reminds me of the joy of play,
With whiskers twitching like prose,
Life's a jest, come what may.

Each second a bubble full of cheer,
Popping and giggling on the floor,
In the messy chaos drawing near,
I find the fun we can't ignore.

Echoes in the Abyss

In the depths, I hear a bell,
Ringing softly, can't quite tell.
Is it wisdom or just a joke?
Lost in laughter, I can't revoke.

Chasing shadows, fall I might,
Tripping on a shoe, what a sight!
Food for thought or just for lunch?
Life's odd puzzles in a crunch.

I search for gold, find only dust,
Chuckle in confusion, it's a must.
Every answer feels like play,
Fooling around, I drift away.

With questions swirling like a stew,
I ponder hard, then lose a shoe.
Is it clarity that I lack?
Maybe life just wants to snack.

In the Shadow of Purpose

A shadow dances, bold and spry,
It tells me jokes, oh me, oh my!
I try to chase it down the lane,
But it just giggles, what a pain.

"Mittens on a cat?" it yells,
"Or flying cows with chocolate swells?"
I scratch my head and scratch some more,
Who's in charge? I need a score.

The candle's lit, but we get lost,
In silly dreams, we wander, tossed.
A purpose found gets lost in play,
As socks go missing, day by day.

What's it all for? Let's grab a drink,
I'll buy a round, we just might think.
If nonsense reigns, then let it be,
At least it's fun, you'll agree with me.

Whispers of Meaning

Whispers linger in the breeze,
Telling tales of flying cheese.
"Why so serious?" shouts the sun,
Let's dance and laugh, that's more fun!

I ponder deep, but not too much,
Carrots wear hats, oh what a touch!
Life's like a jazz band on the run,
Hitting wrong notes, yet it's so fun.

What's the secret? No idea,
But joy can swim like a happy deer.
Meaning hides in a giggly face,
Let's embrace this silly race!

Tickle the clock, it laughs with glee,
Time wobbles like a cup of tea.
Let's toast to joy and dizzy spins,
That's the way this life begins.

Mosaic of Moments

Bits and pieces on the floor,
Chasing ducks, and what's in store?
Life's a puzzle, missing parts,
Arranging chaos, mashing hearts.

Bread on Tuesday, what a feast,\nThat moldy slice, a grimy beast.
Yet laughter bursts, we roll with it,
Like jellybeans, let's never quit.

I write in crayon, splashing bold,
Tales of unicorns wrapped in gold.
Will it matter in the end?
Maybe it's just about the trend.

So gather 'round, let's raise a cheer,
For silly times and snacks we steer.
In the mess, we find the glow,
Life's a dance, let's steal the show.

Navigating the Now

In a world where time just flies,
I trip on shoelaces, oh what a surprise!
Coffee spills, my shirt's a mess,
But hey, that's all part of the quest.

I search for wisdom in my sock drawer,
Finding snacks I forgot before.
The calendar says it's Wednesday again,
Who knew life was a game of pretend?

With every sigh, and every laugh,
I ponder on my chosen path.
Do I need a map or just my phone?
Sometimes it's fun to roam alone.

So here I stand, in ridiculous grace,
With a perplexing smile upon my face.
I may not know what's next in line,
But I'll sip my tea and feel just fine.

Beneath the Surface of Today

The sun shines bright, but where's my hat?
Oh look, a squirrel! I'll chase that brat.
He stole my snack, it seems so unfair,
Life's twists and turns, they're everywhere.

I browse through emails, lost in my thoughts,
Wondering if coffee's really what I sought.
Then a cat walks by, a fluffy muse,
And suddenly, I feel unexcused.

With socks that clash, and hair awry,
I laugh at how I let time fly.
Life's high stakes, a comedy show,
Yet here I am, putting on a show.

Each moment fleeting, like a game of charades,
I dance through chaos, making cascades.
So here's to today, with all its quirks,
In the grand plot of life, I'm on the works!

Chasing Fleeting Shadows

I run in circles, pretending to sprint,
Chasing shadows like a playful hint.
The sun plays tricks, it shifts and bends,
Yet laughter echoes, with all my friends.

I lose my keys, they vanish with glee,
And wonder if my sanity is free.
The dog looks at me, judging my plight,
'Just throw the ball!', he seems to invite.

With ice cream dripping down my hand,
I ponder if life's just a funny band.
Tunes of laughter and awkward tunes,
Life's a circus, under the moon.

So here I am, with a silly grin,
Chasing shadows, let the fun begin.
In this mysterious light and fade,
True joy is found in the games we played.

A Journey to the Heart

I packed my dreams in a colorful bag,
Hitched a ride on a cheerful stag.
We laughed at worries, waved at the clouds,
In this journey, life is fun, not loud.

With each step forward, I trip on my feet,
While humming a tune that's one big repeat.
The road twists and turns like a wobbly kite,
But hey, who's worried? I'll be alright!

I found a map, but it made no sense,
Full of doodles and childish defense.
But in the mess, I hear a voice,
Whispering softly to make a choice.

So here we go, with snacks all around,
With hearts wide open, let laughter abound.
Life's not a race, it's a joyful dash,
I'll take my time, let the moments splash.

Labyrinth of Reflections

In a maze of mirrors, oh what a sight,
I see ten of me, and it feels just right.
With each twist and turn, I lose my way,
Maybe I'm here just to laugh and play.

The sign says 'Exit,' I'll just ignore,
This funhouse vibe, who could ask for more?
Chasing my shadow, it gives me a grin,
Maybe the journey is where the fun begins.

The Echo Chamber of Hope

In a room full of echoes, I shout my plea,
'Life's just a game, come laugh with me!'
The walls just chuckle, what a fine crew,
They bounce back my dreams, all warped and askew.

Every crazy thought, a melody sings,
Who needs the wisdom that adulthood brings?
With every debacle, I find a new tune,
Life's a big dance, and I'm lost in the swoon.

Unseen Connections

I trip over shoelaces, oh what delight,
Invisible strings pull me left and right.
Each step a misstep, a slip and a slide,
Turns out confusion is quite a fun ride.

Connected to laughter, to joy and to glee,
I'll dance with the shadows, just wait and see!
Life's quirky twists, they keep me amused,
Perhaps it's chaos that leaves me unbruised.

Life's Chalice of Wonders

Sipping from a chalice of fizzy bright cheer,
Sipping lemonade, my worries can clear.
The toast is a wink, and laughter the wine,
In this quirky banquet, the stars brightly shine.

With each clink of glasses, a giggle takes flight,
Swirling through chaos, let's revel in light.
Cheers to bad puns and the friends we adore,
In this banquet of life, who could ask for more?

Echoes of Existence

Woke up this morn, the sun was bright,
Coffee in hand, I felt just right.
But where's that spark, that missing fire?
Turns out my sock's the real empire!

I search for wisdom in pizza crust,
Toppings and flavors, I trust.
If cheese is the answer, I'll never know,
As I munch away, just watching the show.

The cat's a sage, gives me a glance,
While pondering life, I take a chance.
But I'm lost in thoughts of yesterday's news,
Oh wait, it's just my mismatched shoes!

In this circus of joys and little woes,
We dance in circles, in silly shows.
So join me, friend, in this jolly jest,
Together we'll figure out the rest!

Searching for Tomorrow's Dawn

The sun tries hard to rise and shine,
But I just want to sip my wine.
With pancakes flipping, what's my goal?
Finding lost keys in a butter bowl!

Each morning I wake, it's an escape,
To discover what mischief I can make.
Maybe it's there, under the bed,
Or in a cereal box, who knows ahead?

I seek revelations in cereal shapes,
Daydreaming of castles built by apes.
Bananas in pajamas have a grand say,
In this wacky puzzle of the day!

With coffee and laughter, let's chart a course,
For giggles and joy—what a mighty force!
Together we ponder, with brains in a whirl,
Like socks in a dryer, we dance and twirl!

In Pursuit of Purpose

What's the reason behind all this fuss?
Is it finding lost change or simply a bus?
With each tiny moment, I seek a clue,
But all I find is last week's stew!

In search of my purpose, I gave it a try,
By training a hamster to jump high.
But it turns out he prefers to nap,
So much for wisdom in a cute little flap.

Life's like a riddle wrapped in a snack,
One bite away from a glorious whack.
I'll enjoy the ride, in pizza I trust,
Making sense of madness, it's a must!

With popcorn clouds and silly thoughts,
A quest for meaning, or so it's sought.
Let's laugh out loud, take naps in the sun,
In this glorious chase, we'll have some fun!

Whispers of a Winding Path

On this path I wander, who knows where it leads?
In a garden of socks, I tend to the weeds.
With flowers of laughter blooming around,
A punchline awaits, any luck to be found?

I tripped on a thought, landed in cheese,
With a chuckle and grin, I'm eager to please.
The purpose is foggy, like toast in the mist,
But a morning giggle surely can't be missed!

In search of some meaning in a banana peel,
I slide through my dreams, what a wild reel!
The whispers of giggles in the air,
Lead to silly stumbles without a care.

So here I sit, with fries on my plate,
Asking the universe, "What's next on my fate?"
With each nibble and chuckle, let's embrace,
This winding adventure, a comical race!

The Tapestry of Be-ing

Life's a quilt of silly threads,
Each stitch a laugh, the needle spreads.
A pop of color here and there,
We all wear patterns, none compare.

Blend the blues with shades of glee,
A patchwork dog with one lost knee.
The quirks we cherish, the joys that twine,
In this grand fabric, we all align.

Glimmers of Truth

In mirrors held up to our grins,
Truth winks back through cheeky spins.
It juggles jokes and plays the fool,
A bubble bath, but no swimming pool.

Shining bright in silly dance,
Life's oddities, our best romance.
With every slip and every trip,
We find the gold beneath the quip.

Awakening to Wonder

Awake with giggles at dawn's first light,
The toaster pops, a silly sight.
Coffee spills in rhythmic cheer,
A dance of mugs, our morning beer.

Curious cats and wobbling dogs,
They teach us laughter, no need for hogs.
In the chaos of breakfast bliss,
Every moment's a giggly kiss.

The Road Less Traveled

There's a road where rubber chickens lay,
With laughter signs guiding the way.
Each step we take, a comedic slip,
A merry-go-round, a joyful trip.

Frogs in tuxedos might greet your eye,
While squirrels navigate the sky.
And if you trip on a banana peel,
Wipe the grin off and strike a wheel.

The Canvas of Existence

Splashes of joy, drips of despair,
We paint with laughter, with a little flair.
Colors collide in a splendid mess,
Who knew existence could be such a jest?

Life's a parade of odd little quirks,
With clowns and jests that always work.
A jigsaw puzzle missing some pieces,
Still fits together as joy never ceases!

When Time Stands Still

I paused to ponder, my coffee grew cold,
Seconds ticked like stories untold.
Tick-tock mocks with a cheeky grin,
Is this where the fun and nonsense begins?

In the hallway of clocks, I take a detour,
Two left feet on a dance floor unsure.
When time stands still, we forget to fret,
And life becomes a whimsical pet!

Dreams on the Horizon

Chasing bright dreams like a kite in the sky,
With a little tug, up, up they fly.
But windy days bring a humorous fall,
Dancing with clouds, we giggle and sprawl.

The horizon winks, as if in on the joke,
"Try to catch dreams!" it whimsically spoke.
But dreams wear capes, dodging hands that grasp,
Yet we laugh at the chase - oh what a gasp!

Invitations to Awakening

Morning coffee, a warm hug of light,
Invitations flutter, oh what a sight!
"Awake!" they shout from the fridge and the bed,
With eggs doing tango while the toast is spread.

Each day is a party, with clatter and cheer,
Rugged slippers dancing, no room for fear.
Life nudges and winks, "Join the delight!"
So let's roll with the day, and hold on tight!

Dance of Ephemera

In a world of fleeting crumbs,
We twirl like lost marbles,
Chasing giggles in the air,
With socks that don't match, we're stable.

We trip on thoughts of grandeur,
While sipping coffee with glee,
Our plans are just doodles,
On napkins, wild and free.

Life's a wobbly jig of flair,
With shoes that squeak and squeal,
We dance through each nutty affair,
To a beat that feels surreal.

So grab a friend, let's shuffle loud,
In this circus of bright daydreams,
We'll crown ourselves the happy crowd,
Waving nonsense like sunbeams.

Conversations with Tomorrow

Tomorrow whispers secrets sweet,
While we're stuck in yesterday's mess,
It giggles at our silly feat,
Like socks that never find their dress.

We chat with cups of coffee bold,
Discussing plans to change the game,
But end up laughing, stories told,
Of mishaps that could earn us fame.

It rolls its eyes at our designs,
As we trip through our winding fate,
Yet somehow still, the sun still shines,
And laughter turns to something great.

So let's toast to our muddled chats,
With tea bags brewing dreams anew,
For in the soup of life, we prance,
Content to play, with joy in view.

Everyday Mysteries

Why does toast land butter-side down?
And where do all the lost socks go?
In this riddle we wear a frown,
While solving puzzles, side by show.

We ponder life in funny ways,
As tacos twirl 'round in our heads,
With laundry piles that spark dismay,
And pillow dreams where logic dreads.

What if bubbles have their own rules?
And fish think we're the oddest sight?
We laugh at fate and play the fools,
On trails where chaos feels so right.

So join my quest for goofy truth,
As we leap through the unknown bright,
We'll wear our laughter like a tooth,
In this dance of odd delight.

The Palette of Our Days

Life's a canvas, splattered wide,
With colors borrowed from our laughs,
We paint with joy, we paint with pride,
Creating quirks and friendly gaffs.

With brushes made of clumsy dreams,
We sketch our worlds in silly strokes,
Each hue a tale, or so it seems,
Comics born of jests and jokes.

A splash of hope, a stroke of fun,
A pinch of chaos, what a show!
We color outside, a portal run,
Where silly spirits freely flow.

So let's mix shades with mirth anew,
In our gallery of carefree play,
Like artists mad, we dare to pursue,
The whims of life, come what may!

Letters to Tomorrow

Dear Tomorrow, can you see,
All the chaos surrounding me?
I sent my dreams with a stamp of glee,
But they bounced back, just like a bee.

I wrote about my plans so grand,
But they slipped away, like grains of sand.
Did you lose my letters, or misplace the band?
I hope you're dancing, just don't misunderstand.

Every day feels like a game,
Where I'm the pawn, but who's to blame?
I'll send you jokes instead of shame,
And hope you smile, that's my claim to fame.

So here's to laughter, here's to cheer,
To finding answers that seem unclear.
If life's a riddle, then let's steer,
And send our worries far from here.

Threads of Connection

In a world where we weave and twine,
Finding laughter in the simplest line.
I dropped my phone, it fell with a whine,
Then tripped on my joy, like a clumsy design.

With every message I send, I grin,
Sending memes to check if you're in.
Tangled in threads, we laugh at our sin,
Who knew connecting could feel like a win?

E-mail dings and texts do pop,
Like popcorn waiting for the flip-flop.
Let's share our tales, and never stop,
For in every thread, we're bound to swap.

So raise a glass to the moments we share,
To the funny things that lay out bare.
Through every glitch and jest, take care,
We're all threads in a fabric most rare.

Reflections in Still Water

I stared at the pond, so clear and wide,
Where ducks quack secrets, and fish like to hide.
They must be laughing at me, full of pride,
As I ponder life's riddle, and what's on the ride.

Every ripple shows a glimpse of the jest,
Is it wisdom or madness that we should test?
I tossed in a coin, hoping for the best,
But it sank like my hopes, just like the rest.

The frogs croak tales like stand-up shows,
While lily pads become my comic prose.
Nature's humor is where intrigue grows,
If only we'd listen, it surely flows.

So let's splash joy in that mirror of blue,
Finding humor in what we think we knew.
Life's just a joke, with laughter in view,
Let's dance by the water, just me and you.

A Map of Hidden Treasures

With a map in my hand and a grin on my face,
I'm on a quest, in a hurried race.
X marks the spot, but what's the case?
Maybe it's hidden in a pinch of grace.

I search for gold, but what do I find?
Old socks, some gum, and a cat that's unkind.
Each clue leads me round, still blissfully blind,
But laughter is wealth—the best you can bind.

I thought I'd discover a fortune untold,
Instead, I unearthed some stories of old.
Riches can't measure the joy I behold,
In the treasure of moments, my heart has consoled.

So here's to maps that lead us astray,
Where the real gems lie in the games that we play.
With laughter our compass, come what may,
We'll treasure each moment, come night or day.

An Atlas of Questions

Why does my sock disappear,
In the wash it seems to steer?
Maps drawn with spaghetti lines,
And lost keys hide in secret shrines.

Do fish in tanks have great talks?
Do they giggle when someone knocks?
When clouds drift by with thoughts so sweet,
Is it a parade, or is it a cheat?

Is toast truly meant to be burnt?
Or just a lesson sharply learnt?
If time flies, where is my plane?
I'll catch it next time, I'm not in vain.

Are jokes just scribbled on the breeze?
Do they tickle trees like tease?
In this mystery, a treasure trove,
I laugh and skip — where's the grove?

Notes from the Edge

Woke up today, what's the plan?
Is it coffee, or 'willy-nilly' ban?
Lost in lists of things to do,
Maybe naps will make me new?

A sandwich, a smoothie, or a feast?
How about a quirky little beast?
Pet rocks that grant wishes of fun,
Or chase sunsets till the day is done?

Shall I dance with shadows on the wall?
Or hold a meeting for my cat and doll?
The edge is a place where giggles grow,
And seriousness bends — just go with the flow.

Some notes scribbled on a napkin here,
Say "pick the laughter, ditch the fear!"
In this symphony of vibrant shouts,
The signs of joy are what life's about.

Compass of the Soul

My compass spins — is it north again?
Or now I find I'm lost in zen?
With laughter guiding every step,
And happy thoughts in every rep.

Should I measure joy in gummy bears?
Or chase the sun like a game of flares?
With giggles that can light the dark,
A light-hearted quest, not just a lark!

Whispers of ice cream after rain,
Or bubble baths to ease the brain?
My soul's mischievous little dance,
Says "take a risk — give life a chance!"

The compass wobbles, that's okay,
For joy never seems to stray.
Just follow the rhythm of your giggle,
And embrace the chaos with a wiggle!

Fragments of Forever

In a land where socks unite,
Laughter echoes day and night.
Fragments scatter, dreams take flight,
As we juggle joy like it's a sprite.

Whispers swirl in silly jokes,
Ticklish secrets, hidden blokes.
With every laugh, the world transforms,
As happy chaos breaks the norms.

Here's to picture frames that dance,
To silly socks in a quirky prance.
Each moment's like a watercolor stain,
Running high while we break the chain.

So gather your fragments, paint them bright,
In this tapestry of sheer delight.
For in the end, we shine and glow,
It's the giggles gathered that truly flow.

Fleeting Footprints

We danced on a whim, just to see,
If laughter could float like a leaf on the sea.
A squirrel popped by, wearing its crown,
Mocking our search while bouncing around.

Each step that we took was a wobbly trail,
Like penguins on ice or a snail with a sail.
We chased silly dreams in a world quite absurd,
Just hoping to catch what was already stirred.

With donuts and coffee, we planned our grand goals,
Mapping out futures with jelly-filled rolls.
But every new twist was a fork in the road,
And GPS said, "Just lighten the load!"

So if you get lost in this whimsical race,
Recall wandering 's fun, just embrace the space.
For footprints may fade, but the giggles will stay,
In this circus of life where we frolic and play.

In Quest of Essence

We searched for the key in a jar full of bees,
Thought wisdom could buzz like a sweet summer breeze.
Swapping our secrets with a wise old toad,
Who croaked about carrots on the long, winding road.

A cat in a hat claimed he'd know all the tricks,
He charmed us with riddles and some clever flicks.
But as we all laughed at his puzzling tale,
He slipped in a puddle, oh how we'd wail!

We plotted our course with crayons and maps,
Sketching our thoughts through giggles and claps.
Yet somehow we found that the treasure was small,
Just tiny moments that made us feel tall.

So toast to the journey, let nonsense be light,
For the essence we seek is in laughter, not fright.
In this treasure hunt filled with quirky delight,
Our quest is the fun—no end in sight!

Between the Lines of Time

Caught in a loop where the clocks just melt,
We laughed at the sandwiches that no one had dealt.
Time passed like turtles on an old winding road,
While we chased after seconds—oh, the stories they showed!

A penguin in spectacles pointed the way,
Said, "Life's not a race, it's a pancake buffet!"
With each syrupy moment we savored the taste,
Of chaos and giggles, not a second to waste.

Between silly scribbles and doodles galore,
We discovered the joy that we couldn't ignore.
Each tick and each tock was a humorous song,
Reminding us gently that being is strong.

So here's to the moments that twist and that flip,
The laughter, the joy on this paradox trip.
When we write our own lines in this whimsical rhyme,
We'll find that the fun is what's treasure in time!

Finding Clarity in Chaos

In the midst of the whirlwind where socks chase their mates,
We danced through confusion, creating our fates.
With bubbles and giggles, we caught the wild breeze,
And juggled our worries like clumsy sweet peas.

We spilled all our thoughts like marbles on floors,
And turned every frown into slapstick galore.
As penguins wore bow ties and dachshunds would prance,
We found joy in the mess in our zany romance.

Amidst all the hiccups and zany goofs made,
We surfed on the chaos, our laughter displayed.
For clarity blinks in a ticklish dance,
Where fun is the lens through which we enhance.

So if life gets tangled in misfit surprise,
Just giggle and waltz, let your spirit arise.
For in each burst of laughter and wild, silly spin,
We'll find that the joy is where we begin!

Pages of a Hidden Book

Once lost in a dusty nook,
I found a page, a quirky hook.
It spoke of shoes that danced at night,
And cats that wore a top hat tight.

Bizarre tales of grand escapades,
In a world where nothing persuades.
From garden gnomes to ducks in ties,
I chuckled hard, 'neath moonlit skies.

Each chapter flipped, a quirky feat,
Gave life to laughter, oh so sweet.
Pages turned, with giggles loud,
Found joy in chaos, far from proud.

So here I sit, a book in hand,
Reading nonsense, life unplanned.
With every laugh, a secret discovered,
In this strange book, I'm covered and uncovered.

Voices of the Unspoken

Whispers float in the morning air,
From squirrels chatting without a care.
They gossip 'bout nuts and daring feats,
While I sip coffee, enjoying treats.

Invisible words dance on the breeze,
In a language only the birds perceive.
A crow remarks on life's funny mess,
While I nod along, feeling quite blessed.

A frog croaks tales of days gone by,
Of feasts of flies and mud pie high.
They ribbit with laughter, sing with glee,
In their world, joy is wild and free.

So I join in, with my laugh so loud,
Listening close, feeling so proud.
In the silence, humor's sweet embrace,
In this merry choir, I've found my place.

Lanterns along the Way

Stumbling through life, like a blindfolded fool,
I tripped on a lantern, right by the pool.
It painted my path with a golden hue,
Revealing the laughter I never knew.

Around each corner, a glow so bright,
Showed me where I'd misplaced my light.
With giggles echoing in the night air,
I danced with shadows, devoid of a care.

Each flicker of hope brought fresh delight,
Like finding a sandwich at a pizza fight.
With lanterns aglow, I ventured forth,
Chasing the joy that felt so worth.

So in this journey, clumsy yet bright,
I find my way, guided by light.
And with every glow, and every cheeky grin,
I laugh at the chaos, let the fun begin!

Harvesting Joy

In fields of giggles, I sow my seeds,
Watering laughter with ridiculous deeds.
I dance with spinach, sing with peas,
Among the carrots, my soul finds ease.

Each berry plucked, a sweet surprise,
Under a sunlit, forgiving sky.
Jokes sprout like flowers, all blooming bright,
While veggies chuckle, oh what a sight!

With baskets full, I head to the fair,
Trading joy and jest with those who dare.
The harvest season, a comical spree,
Where every laugh adds to the glee.

So here I stand, in this field of cheer,
Gathering smiles from far and near.
In this funny dance of life I play,
I find my joy in each silly display.

Traces of Meaning in the Ordinary

I spilled coffee on my shirt today,
Does that mean I'm meant to play?
Maybe life's clues are all around,
In every laugh and silly sound.

A cat that naps upon my lap,
Whispers secrets in a nap.
Where does meaning like to hide?
In the giggles we can't bide.

Missing keys and lost remote,
Is this a life's little joke I wrote?
The quest for purpose, oh what a mess,
Perhaps it's just to wear my dress!

So here I am, with crumbs to show,
In the chaos, do you think I'll grow?
Perhaps in chocolate or pizza pie,
Is where all the wisdom truly lies!

The Compass of the Heart

My heart beats like a drummer's show,
With every skip, it starts to flow.
Finding paths in quirky ways,
Like walking ducks on sunny days.

A map that leads to the last slice,
Of pizza topped with too much spice!
Could that be it? Oh, what a feat!
A compass set for greasy treats!

Directions scribbled on a napkin,
Point to places we keep clapping.
With every step, we dance around,
To beats of joys that we have found.

So if you wander, take my hand,
We'll find delight where we once planned.
Through laughter shared and silly quotes,
The heart's compass, it truly floats!

Shadows of Forgotten Dreams

In shadows where old dreams reside,
A plushy panda is my guide.
Forgotten things from long ago,
Like socks that vanish in a show.

Dusty wishes on the shelf,
Are they just reflections of myself?
Did I once want that purple hat?
Or was it all just a silly spat?

I chased a rainbow in my sleep,
To find the pot of gold, so deep.
But all I found was spilled ice cream,
And in that chaos, I found a dream.

So here's to shadows wanting light,
Let's dance with them, hold them tight.
For every silly, lost esteem,
Might just be the start of a new theme!

Between Here and Forever

I'm stuck between a rock and cheese,
Where every crumb's meant to please.
Let's take a journey, side by side,
Through moments of joy we cannot hide.

In giggles and bumps along the way,
We'll find our truth in a child's play.
With ice cream cones and sunny skies,
Are we not wise in our own ties?

Sometimes it seems we're lost for sure,
Yet laughter's map is the perfect cure.
In every stumble, let's just beam,
For between here, we find the dream.

So grab a friend, let's just explore,
Each little giggle, each open door.
For in the mess of what we seek,
Is humor's truth, and that's not bleak!

A Journey Through Moments

Woke up today, spilled my tea,
Found a sock that's lost at sea.
Chased a dream, but it fled so fast,
Guess I'll settle for toast at last.

Every corner holds a quirky face,
Stumbling on laughter, a secret place.
Sticking gum on the shoe of fate,
How this journey can be so great!

Frogs serenade in the summer breeze,
Taking tips from the dancing trees.
Life's a maze, oh what a twist,
Just when you think you've got the gist.

Lemonade stands and wildflower fields,
Chasing joy with amusing shields.
At the end of the road, what's the score?
Smiles collected, let's grab some more!

Life's Hidden Treasures

In my pocket, a crumpled map,
Says 'X' marks the spot for a nap.
A treasure chest? Just old receipts,
Monopoly money and socked-up beats.

Found a penny, thought I was rich,
Turns out it's just for a witch's pitch.
Life's treasures, mostly like old shoes,
Tales of adventure in wrinkled news.

Chocolate cake crumbs on my shirt,
A glorious feast of dessert dirt.
Wandering through the aisles of time,
Stumbling sometimes, but isn't it prime?

Lift the lid, let the laughter in,
Searching for gems where the fun begins.
The real treasure is found with friends,
Invisible joy that never ends!

Unraveled Threads of Time

Time's a yarn ball, all in a mess,
Pull one string, you'll never guess.
A cat pounces, the clock chimes loud,
Spinning stories that wow the crowd.

Wrinkles of laughter on life's page,
Tickles of worry, turn up the gauge.
Pull out a fiber, watch it unwind,
Seek the lost moments, you'll surely find.

Kites flying high in a windy craze,
Tangled thoughts in a happy daze.
Moments slip through like sand in hand,
But laughter's the glue that makes us a band.

Wrap it up with a cheerful bow,
Marching to rhythms only we know.
Though the stitches may fray with time,
Dance in the chaos, life is sublime!

Questing the Quiet Answers

Sipping tea with a side of quirks,
Seeking answers like a catfish lurks.
Is it under the bed? In a shoe?
Or perhaps in the next sneeze, who knew?

Puzzles cracked with each hit or miss,
Finding wisdom in a playful kiss.
Tickling thoughts like a feather's tease,
The quiet answers come with ease.

A squirrel's debate on a tree branch,
What's the question? Here's my chance.
Dance like no one is seeing you,
Even the trees smile at what you do.

In the giggles, in the sighs,
Answers hide in the baby cries.
So let's quest on, chase the bizarre,
Every laugh, a shining star!

Finding Footings in Fog

I wandered through the misty haze,
Searching for my lost keys, you see.
I tripped on air, fell in a daze,
And met a squirrel who laughed at me.

I asked him for directions home,
He pointed and said, 'Just keep it light!'
But then he scampered, gone to roam,
Leaving me in this foggy plight.

I pondered if I'd lost my way,
Maybe I was meant to stay here.
With squirrels plotting, all game and play,
I found my lost sense of cheer.

In clouds of grey, I searched for sense,
But laughter's the only clue I trace.
Life's twists and turns can be immense,
So I'll dance here in this silly place.

Voices Beneath the Surface

In a pond where frogs discuss the day,
I eavesdropped on their croaky chats.
They pondered life in a jumping way,
And occasionally argued over hats.

A duck swam by, quacking like a king,
Saying, 'Why chase dreams on dry ground?'
'Jump in the water, let your heart sing!'
And he splashed around without a sound.

The turtles lounged, all wise and slow,
Sipping tea with a leaf for a cup.
They spilled secrets in the pond's soft flow,
Saying, 'Relax, no need to hurry up!'

Between splashes and croaks, I found delight,
That wisdom hides in puddles and streams.
With laughter echoing throughout the night,
Life's funny when you follow your dreams.

Harvesting the Unexpected

I planted seeds of hopes and dreams,
Expecting veggies, pure and bright.
But grew a garden of silly themes,
Carrots wore hats, what a sight!

Tomatoes danced in the summer sun,
While cabbages hummed a tune so sweet.
I thought gardening should be fun,
So I joined in their whimsical beat.

When harvest came, I filled my sack,
With veggies all dressed up, quite rare.
I laughed and danced, it's quite a hack,
Life's laughter blooms in the oddest fare!

So here's my bounty, both strange and bright,
They might not cook, but they certainly play.
Finding joy in all that's weird and light,
I feast on giggles every day.

When Silence Speaks

In a room where whispers often dwell,
Silence sat up, took a chair with style.
It waved its arms, casting a spell,
And made me giggle with its secret smile.

I asked it why it liked to stand,
It shrugged and made a tick-tock sound.
'Sometimes the quiet lends a hand,
To hear the laughter all around.'

A mouse peeked in, surprised and grinned,
'You hear that, too? It's quite absurd!'
We laughed aloud, our doubts rescinned,
Found joy where once silence was heard.

In quiet times, you may just see,
The funny truths that life can weave.
For in the hush, oh, what glee,
Laughter's echo is hard to believe!

Unraveling the Mysteries

In a maze of socks and keys,
I search for wisdom with such ease.
The cat just stares and licks its paw,
While I contemplate the meaning of a flaw.

I planted seeds in pants, oh dear!
A garden grew, but not quite here.
Tomatoes sprouted in a shoe,
Who knew that gardening could stink so blue?

Each wrinkle hides a little clue,
On why I left the milk out too.
Breading dough, a rising concern,
It's the yeast that knows what I must learn.

With coffee cups in hand, we gloat,
As if we've figured out the boat.
But the boat just circles near the shore,
While we debate which way is more.

The Dance of Existence

Two left feet in a world of grace,
I trip over my very own shoelace.
The rhythm's there, but I've lost the beat,
Still, I dance on, feeling so sweet.

Life's a jig in a wobbly chair,
Where laughter bubbles up in the air.
I spin in circles with absolute glee,
Till I stumble upon my own TV.

A dance-off with my reflection's fun,
We're both confused, pretending to run.
But as I tumble, I hear the sound—
It's joy, bouncing all around!

Twirl around boredom, shake off the dust,
Existence is strange; it's a must.
So grab my hand, let's jig away,
Tomorrow we'll laugh at today!

Beneath the Stars

Under the sky of twinkling cheer,
I ponder if aliens drink root beer.
The night whispers secrets, jokes, and puns,
While we sit counting Saturn's strange runs.

My telescope's a cardboard tube,
Pointing at stars, feeling pretty shrewd.
But wait a sec, that's just a light,
From my neighbor's porch, blinding my sight.

Astrology says I'm a certain sign,
Yet I've lost my keys and my favorite wine.
The stars align, or so they say,
But all I see is a raccoon's ballet!

We laugh at dreams like fishing nets,
Catching the wishes that life forgets.
So here's to cosmic, quirky fun,
When you lose the way, just run with the sun!

Sparks of Intention

Like fireworks in a microwave,
I'm bursting with hopes—I misbehave.
A spark ignites in the toaster's warm glow,
Conceiving plans I barely know.

Intentions scribbled on the back of a napkin,
Reveal a future where we're all rappin'.
A pop, a fizz, and a sudden sway,
Who needs missteps? It's all play!

I wrote a letter to my pillow last night,
Confessed my dreams in a sleepy flight.
It replied with a snore and a soft fluff,
Sparks of intention just aren't enough!

Juggling ideas like bananas in air,
With laughter echoing everywhere.
In the end, it's all just a game,
So let's twist the chances, nothing is plain!

The Silence of Questions

Why do socks disappear in the wash?
Is there a sock thief, or a cruel ambush?
Every question hangs, like a balloon in air,
Drifting around without a single care.

Do you ever wonder why cats love to pick,
The worst time to jump onto your laptop quick?
They stare into screens like they know it all,
While we're just baffled by the latest app's call.

And why do we laugh when we trip on our shoe?
Is it the ground's fault, or just something we do?
Life's a big circus with clowns running wild,
Stepping on toes, like a mischief-maker child.

So bring on the questions, the quirks, and the fun,
We'll dance with confusion 'til the day is done.
In this comical chaos, let's just take a seat,
As we sip our coffee and embrace the sweet beat.

Capturing Fleeting Thoughts

Flitting ideas like butterflies, bright,
They land on your mind, then take off in flight.
You reach for a notepad, but it's out of sight,
And they giggle as they vanish into the night.

Yesterday, I found a thought, oh so grand,
It slipped right through fingers like fine, shifting sand.
I chased it through rooms with a snack in my hand,
Only to find it's been part of a band!

What if we gathered up each tiny whim?
A library filled from porch to the gym.
But then I get dizzy from thoughts that just swim,
In this pool of confusion, I hope I don't trim.

Maybe the trick is to just let them be,
A wild collection of thoughts, just like me.
So when they come knocking, we'll offer a cup,
And laugh at the silliness that fills our ups!

Sunlight on the Path

Skipping along, with shadows in tow,
I dance with the sun, letting worries go.
Each ray is a laugh that tickles my face,
As I roll down the hill, it's a comic embrace.

Are we lost in the woods, or just on a quest?
With squirrels as guides, we're truly blessed.
Chasing our tails, like a puppy so spry,
Who needs a map when you can wing it and fly?

The sunlight flickers, like laughter that plays,
In this world of mischief, in whimsical ways.
With each step I take, it's fun that I sense,
Finding joy in the bumps, what a joy, what a tense!

So bring out your sunnies, and dance through the day,
Let the light guide your giggles, come join in the play.
For in silly moments, life's treasure's revealed,
And in laughter we find what time cannot shield.

In the Midst of Breath

Inhale the giggles, exhale the stress,
Life's a wacky ride, but we're truly blessed.
With each little chuckle, a bubble we blow,
As we tumble through moments that steal the show.

Why take it so seriously, with frowns on our face?
Let's wear silly hats and embrace this wild race.
The world's just a playground with swings and a slide,
And laughter, my friends, is the best thing we've tried.

Breath in the whimsy, exhale all the fuss,
Let's spin like tops, just because — why not us?
In these fleeting seconds, we find our true worth,
When joy dances lightly, we're thankful for mirth.

So here's to the giggles that keep us alive,
In the midst of this chaos, we thrive and we jive.
So hold onto your breath and let laughter ignite,
For the moments we treasure are really a delight!

The Quest for Wholeness

I searched in the fridge for treasure to find,
A leftover pizza seemed quite unrefined.
With mustard and pickles, I made a great feast,
But now I'm questioning what I like least.

They said to be whole, one must really dig deep,
But all that I found was my old phone's beep.
I tripped on my cat, while pondering fate,
Now he's judging me—oh, isn't life great?

In doing the laundry, I found a sock pair,
Worn by my foot—now they don't even care.
Like me, they are lost, perhaps looking for fun,
Together we'd laugh, until I'm done!

So off I will go, with a grin on my face,
The quest for wholeness turns into a race.
To find out if happiness is in my next snack,
Or right under the couch, on the dusty old track!

Embracing the Unknown

I wandered through life with a map made of cheese,
Got lost in a maze of uncertainties, please.
The paths that I chose led to funny mishaps,
Like dogs in tuxedos doing silly lap laps.

I tried to embrace what I'd not yet discovered,
Spilled coffee on plans, what a lovely blunder!
With doughnuts as guides, I followed the sweet,
But the chocolate ones vanished—now that's a defeat!

I met a wise owl, or maybe just fluff,
He hooted some wisdom, but it's still quite tough.
The journey is messy and far from refined,
But laughter's the secret that keeps me aligned.

So here's to the chaos, the joy, and the fun,
Embracing the unknown, oh what have I done?
With sprinkles of courage and giggles galore,
Life's best when it's quirky—can't wait for more!

Migrations of the Mind

My thoughts like the birds took a flight in July,
They landed on beaches, oh my, oh my!
From pondering pickles to giggling at clouds,
Each thought was a party, complete with loud crowds.

I chased after dreams dressed in flip-flop attire,
While minding the gaps and avoiding the mire.
But sometimes they flutter like butterflies shy,
I yell out their names but they just wave goodbye.

Visiting places with names I can't say,
Like "whatchamacallit" or "thingamajig" play.
I scribble my thoughts on the back of my hand,
Hoping one day they'll form a good band.

So here's to the travels of fancy and fun,
To thinking in circles until I can run.
Migrations of mind may seem quite absurd,
But each little giggle sings without word.

In Search of Horizon

I set out for horizon with snacks in my bag,
But tripped on my shoelace, what a silly drag!
With jellybeans bouncing and laughter my guide,
I questioned if I really cared where it would ride.

The sun laughed at me with its big golden glow,
While clouds floated by, putting on a grand show.
"Hey look!" said my friend, "Is that a new trend?"
I nodded and chuckled—we're lost with no end!

With marshmallow dreams and ambitions that fly,
We wandered through life, letting giggles reply.
The journey's made better with dance and a grin,
So onward we march, let the silliness win!

As I search for horizons, it's clear to me now,
They're not some far place, but right here somehow.
In each laugh we share and sweet snacks that we crave,
There's joy in the journey—let's ride this wave!

Collecting Moments of Resonance

I walked through fields of jellybeans,
Hoping for snacks or silly scenes.
But all I found were chips and dip,
And a duck who'd just done a fancy flip.

In corners where shadows dance and twirl,
A rubber chicken gave a silly whirl.
Every giggle that escaped my lips,
Was a moment caught, like candy flips.

I laughed at clouds shaped like old shoes,
And dodged the rain like it had the blues.
Each chuckle felt like an earned reward,
A tasty treat from life's funny hoard.

So here I stand, with laughter in hand,
Collecting moments, each a grain of sand.
With every smile, I build my stash,
In a life that sparkles like a splash.

Unveiling the Hidden Map.

A treasure map was drawn in chalk,
With arrows leading to a squirrel's walk.
Each 'X' marked where snacks dropped low,
As I followed clues to the Great Chip Show.

I asked a cat, who was sipping tea,
'Tell me the secrets of life's decree?'
He nodded once, then took a nap,
Leaving me puzzled, staring at the map.

With a compass made of wiggly worms,
I searched for meaning in funny terms.
But all I found were silly puns,
And ducks on tricycles, playing with guns.

Perhaps the treasure wasn't gold,
But laughter and joy, as I was told.
With squiggly paths, the map was a hoot,
Leading me to a dance with a cute little squirrel.

Searching for Significance

In my quest for weighty truths and tales,
I found a toaster with butterfly sails.
It popped up thoughts toasted just right,
Making breakfast while cranking out light.

A sock puppet claimed he'd know it all,
But lost his voice right after a fall.
While he munched on an old bag of chips,
I scribbled notes of his mighty quips.

I wandered through forests of rubber trees,
Where every breeze tickled my knees.
Amongst the laughter, the silly games,
I sought the meaning, but only found names.

Yet with every found crumb of delight,
I learned that searching felt just right.
Each giggle, each snort, so brightly lit,
Said maybe the answer's in laughter, a bit.

Threads of Existence

I wove together the threads of the day,
With silly yarn that danced in play.
Each loop a laugh, each knot a jest,
Creating a quilt of the very best.

A goldfish sang a tune so sweet,
While I tripped on my own two feet.
With each awkward step, a tale unspooled,
We laughed so hard, we both were schooled.

Pen and paper, my trusty mates,
Wrote all the nonsense that life dictates.
And in the chaos of socks and shoes,
I found the humor in all the blues.

So here's to the threads of silly bliss,
Creating a fabric that life can't miss.
With colors bright and patterns grand,
I stitched my joy with a giggling hand.

Navigating the Unknown

In a maze of socks I wander,
Where's the map, or even the key?
Ducks quack wisdom from the pond,
But their tips are lost on me.

I sip my tea, yet feel so bold,
Chasing dreams that flutter and flip.
A fortune teller made of gold,
Told me not to lose my grip!

Life's a burger, messy and wide,
With ketchup squirted here and there.
I chew my way through each sweet bite,
And wonder if it's wise to care.

With every giggle, I track my steps,
Around the couch and to the stairs.
Did I leave my sanity in the fridge?
Or is it hiding under my chairs?

Footprints on the Sands of Purpose

Footprints stamped on grains of sand,
Yet the tide just laughs and pulls.
I chase a crab that gave me a hand,
But he scuttled off for some rolls.

With a beach ball stuck on my nose,
And sunglasses upside down,
I may not know where life goes,
But I'm the silliest queen in town!

Seagulls plot with cheeky smiles,
Stealing fries from unsuspecting hands.
I throw them crumbs and walk in styles,
Confusing everyone on the sands.

Each splash a giggle, and belly laughs,
My purpose's just a silly game.
So let's doodle paths and bubbly crafts,
While mixing sunshine with a bit of rain!

Reflections in a Still Pond

I gazed into a pond so clear,
And saw my hopes do the cha-cha.
A frog leaped in, with no fear,
Saying, "Life's just a breezy piñata!"

Little ripples dance around,
Each one a laugh, a twist, a zing.
I pondered why I'm pond-bound,
Then tossed in bread to see what it brings.

Fish flip and flop like fancy shoes,
Chasing breadcrumbs, lost in delight.
Every splash, like silly news,
Saying, "Don't worry, you'll be alright!"

So I'll sit here and ponder on,
With turtles joining the froggy spree.
A dance in circles till we yawn,
And splash ourselves with glee!

The Unseen Guidebook

Rumors say a guidebook lies,
Hidden behind my cluttered shelf.
I'd look for it if it weren't a surprise,
That I've lost myself in being myself.

With sticky notes and coffee spills,
I've jotted down my bright ideas.
But most of them are just for thrills,
Like singing off-key to my fears.

The cat seems wise, she gives me glares,
As if she knows the secret code.
Is she my guide through life's affairs?
Or just a fluffball in stealth mode?

So here I am, just doing me,
With life's handbook still misplaced.
I'll follow giggles; they'll set me free,
For joy's the best map, interlaced!

Sketches of a Soul's Desire

In a world of joy and jive,
I sketched a dream, oh so alive.
With crayons bright and silly hats,
I sought my heart 'mongst curious cats.

Through pastry shops and dancing shoes,
I chased the laugh, refused the blues.
I tripped on joy, fell in the cake,
And wondered, was that a big mistake?

I asked a frog to join my quest,
He croaked a tune, said, 'Life's a jest!'
We hopped along, no path in sight,
Embracing chaos, pure delight.

So here's to dreams, both big and small,
To aim for stars and take a fall.
For in the mess, we find our flair,
A little whimsy in the air.

Bending Light Through Love

Love bends like light in a glass jar,
Twisting around, a shining star.
With giggles bright and jokes galore,
It tickles hearts, asks for more.

We danced through puddles, side by side,
Chasing rainbows, our hearts spry.
A squirrel joined in, what a sight,
As love took us to dizzy heights.

We wore our quirks like badges bold,
In a world of stories, both new and old.
With laughter's spark, we found our way,
Bending through darkness, come what may.

So here's to love that makes us grin,
A radiance of joy that lies within.
In every twist, we'll shine and sway,
Forever dancing, come what may.

Fragments of a Grand Design

In a puzzle of life that's oft unclear,
I found some pieces, let out a cheer!
A headless statue, a shoe, a book,
All mixed up in a funny nook.

Each fragment shines, a tale to tell,
Of oops and yikes, oh how they swell.
With mismatched socks and silly cheers,
We built our dreams through childish years.

A toaster talks, a kettle sings,
We craft our joy with everyday things.
In quirky corners, we lose our fuss,
And laugh at life, just not with us.

So here's to life, a grand display,
With all its quirks leading the way.
In fragments true, we'll carve our fate,
With giggles bright, we celebrate.

A Tapestry of Fleeting Time

In the fabric of time, I weave my dreams,
With threads of laughter, or so it seems.
A stitch of love, a knot of fun,
Creating chaos, day by day run.

Each moment's thread, a curious hue,
From ice cream spills to skies so blue.
We yarn and tangle, lose track of hours,
In the madness, bloom like flowers.

As clocks tick louder, we dance with glee,
Spinning tales, wild and free.
With every loop, we find our way,
Laughing at time, come what may.

So let's embrace this quirky loom,
Where joy jumps high and banishes gloom.
For in each thread, we'll find a rhyme,
In a tapestry of fleeting time.

A Journey in Circles

Round and round on this crazy ride,
Chasing tails, nowhere to hide.
With every turn, a laugh we find,
As we search for the treasure, a little blind.

Maps in hand, we roam with glee,
Finding snacks is our main decree.
Yet in this quest, so full of cheer,
We can't recall why we are here.

The compass spins, we giggle loud,
Lost and found in a silly crowd.
Oh, the wisdom we seem to miss,
While leaping about in joyful bliss.

But every twist leads to a treat,
A game of hide and seek, so sweet.
In circles we laugh, in circles we play,
Perhaps it's the journey that brightens the day.

Shimmering Possibilities

Under bright lights, the disco spins,
With daft dancers showing off their sins.
We twirl and whirl, all glimmer and shine,
Chasing sparkles, feeling just fine.

Possibilities spark in the quirky night,
Where everyone claims they've got it right.
But really, who knows what's on the list?
Is it wisdom or just another twist?

We toast to dreams wrapped in glitter,
Each soft chuckle, a joyful flitter.
From clumsy moves to vibrant strife,
We laugh at the nonsense that colors our life.

With each sip, a new path appears,
More comical than shedding our fears.
In shimmering nights, so bizarre and bright,
We stumble towards what feels just right.

Awakening in the Ordinary

Waking up to socks that don't match,
Coffee spills with a splish and a splatch.
Ordinary days, packed with delight,
Finding joy in the mundane sight.

The toaster sings as it pops away,
Brocolli in pajamas—what a display!
In the chaos, we grin ear to ear,
As breakfast turns to a comedic affair.

Chasing dust bunnies like furry pets,
In our little world, there're no regrets.
Simple pleasures create a fest,
Awakening hearts, at our funny best.

As we march through the banal grind,
It's the giggles and snorts that bind.
In every moment, a spark we embrace,
Finding treasure in the silliest place.

The Forgotten Corners

In dusty nooks where secrets sleep,
A lost sock whispers, 'Don't make me weep!'
Under the couch, forgotten remains,
A treasure trove of our quirky gains.

Old books piled, gathering dust,
Reminders of dreams, adjust they must.
Covering cobwebs of laughter and tears,
In forgotten corners, we face our fears.

The fridge hums a nostalgic tune,
With expired yogurt like a cartoon.
Late-night snacks, much to our surprise,
Behind those jars, lies life's sweet guise.

So here's to the places we tend to ignore,
With each little find, let's laugh some more.
In forgotten corners, we dance and cheer,
Finding joy in the places held dear.

Intersections of Hope and Doubt

In the maze, I find a snack,
Hope says, "Stay!" while Doubt pulls back.
I trip on dreams that laugh and tease,
Amidst the chaos, I find my breeze.

Crossing paths with fate so sly,
I ask the stars, but they just sigh.
A squirrel offers wisdom from a branch,
"Life's a giggle, take a chance!"

I think I'm lost, but maybe found,
In the rhythms of absurd sound.
My compass spins, a silly show,
Feeling aimless – or is it flow?

With every stumble, I claim my crown,
Hope wears sunglasses, while Doubt wears a frown.
Around each corner, a joke unfolds,
Laughter's currency, worth more than gold.

A Gentle Push Against the Flow

I paddle sideways in a stream,
Fish laugh at my quirky dream.
The current says, "Go this way!"
But who needs rules in this cliché?

With every splash, I make a scene,
The ducks all stare – I'm the queen!
Who knew the river could be a stage,
For every fool with a blank page?

I'd rather float with my special flair,
Than race upstream with a worried air.
A leaf joins in, it swirls around,
In this comedy, I'm glory bound.

With laughter echoing, I take a dive,
In this wild flow, I feel alive.
No one can tell me how to glide,
With joy as my navigator, I slide!

Echoes of What Could Be

In the hall of missed chances, I stroll,
Trying to find my one true goal.
The echoes chuckle, make it clear,
That's it's the journey we should hold dear.

A whisper says, "Why not try?"
While the echoes laugh and slyly fly.
A rubber chicken comes to play,
Reminding me that I'm okay.

I chase shadows of my past days,
Twisting laughter in silly ways.
In every corner, a thought takes flight,
Dancing in the glow of soft twilight.

So here I stand, a jester proud,
In the echoes, I dance, I'm loud.
What could be is but a jest,
And in the punchline, I am blessed.

The Dance of Serendipity

In a crowded room, I trip and twirl,
Accidental bumps make laughter swirl.
A dance of fate, all out of sync,
Who knew chaos could be this pink?

Twists and turns, I find a friend,
As life's odd rhythms start to blend.
With every misstep, a giggle erupts,
In this quirky waltz, we lift the cups!

A cat walks by with a sassy strut,
Nudging me gently with a playful cut.
Together we leap, defying the beat,
The world's a circus, and we're on repeat!

So come and join this silly spree,
In the dance of chance, feel wild and free.
What serendipity shows in its twist,
Is a happy tune that can't be missed!

www.ingramcontent.com/pod-product-compliance
Lightning Source LLC
Chambersburg PA
CBHW072147200426
43209CB00051B/813